Pubs and Pub Signs

A Colourmaster Publication

Colourmaster International (Photo Precision Limited)
Caxton Road St. Ives Huntingdon England

Acknowledgements

The publishers express their gratitude to the
following individuals and organisations:–
The Brewers' Society and Whitbread & Company
Ltd. for permission to reproduce illustrations
of pub signs. Watney Mann Ltd. for
photographs of some of their houses.
Mrs. Margaret Mainprize for permission to
include the illustration of the Three Mariners.
Helpful factual information has been supplied
by Trust Houses Forte Ltd., Bass Charrington
Ltd., Mr. R. J. Webber, Mr. J. W. Gregory and
Mr. N. R. Draycott.

ISBN 0 85933 105 9

Published by Colourmaster International (Photo Precision Limited)
Caxton Road St. Ives Huntingdon England

Some readers may be surprised to learn that ale was being brewed here before the Romans landed and that ale houses were trading before the Normans came. The pub has a long and proud tradition. A unique and seemingly indestructible British institution, it is the envy of the rest of the world.

Among our 70,000 licensed premises there are some that are set in dismal surroundings and are nondescript in themselves but there are also many of outstanding architectural interest and importance, located in some of the most beautiful parts of Britain. Some of them have fascinating links with Church and State while others have associations with famous and also with infamous figures from many walks of life—artists and men of letters, highwaymen and smugglers, cranks and criminals, some of them notable, others notorious, all of them interesting.

Our pubs are an integral part of the British way of life and the ensuing pages are designed to provide an interesting illustrated background to the story and to say something about the origins of the signs which nearly all of them continue to carry.

Pubs

No one can say when or where the first pub was founded but we had mastered the art of brewing ale long before the Romans arrived on our shores.

The ingredients consisted of malt, which was made mainly from barley, water and yeast and it was not until as late as the fifteenth century that an improved beverage, later to become beer, was perfected by the introduction of hops. Referring to ale, the Roman historian Pliny the Elder, was able to moralise about the whole world being *'addicted to drunkenness; the perverted ingenuity of man has given even to water the power of intoxicating where wine is not procurable. Western nations intoxicate themselves by means of moistened grain'*.

Five hundred years later and after the influences of Christianity had reached Northern Europe, Saint David was busily proselytizing and founding monasteries in Wales. He was obviously concerned about the drinking habits of the local populace and felt inspired enough to decree: *'Those who get drunk through ignorance must do penance fifteen days, if through negligence forty days, if through contempt, three quarantains'*.

It would appear that the situation worsened and by the year 695 we hear of the King of Kent ordering that if any priest *'is too drunk to discharge his duty, he shall abstain from his ministrations, pending a decision from the bishop'*.

During the years leading up to the Norman invasion there appear to have been a number of ale-houses in existence in most towns, villages and even alongside some of the old Roman roads, which by now had

In the ancient ecclesiastical town of Dorchester (Oxon), the Guest House, used to accommodate pilgrims and travellers, is the only part of the monastic buildings to have escaped demolition in the 16th century. The nearby inn, The George, was originally a brew-house used by monks at the Abbey.

probably fallen into considerable neglect and disrepair. The publican lived close to the ale hut and he was, of course, also the brewer.

Travellers were able to identify ale-houses by the long wooden poles which had been adapted from the Romans, who had long ago used various trade signs. Archaeologists have excavated a number of these early emblems from the ruins of Pompeii and Herculaneum. Some of the early ale-houses also sold wine and an evergreen hanging outside the building was used to denote this.

It must come as no surprise to hear of the strong arm of the law taking an interest in the spread of these drinking establishments and under the rule of King Edgar (959-75) it was decreed that each village should only be allowed one ale-house. No doubt a number of ale-houses were forced to close because of this measure and a new innovation aimed at curbing drunkenness required the fitting of pegs at regular intervals inside drinking horns and prohibiting the drinker from going beyond a fresh mark at each draught. However, this well intentioned idea failed to make any drastic improvement and in fact actually encouraged competitive drinking bouts. In 1102 it was ruled that priests should not indulge in 'drinking to pegs' and it is said that the expression of 'taking someone down a peg' had its origins here.

The Church was also taking restrictive measures against the misuse of alcohol and various ecclesiastical canons were issued. *'Let no priest drink at taverns as secular people do. Nor ought men to drink or eat intemperately . . . and drink to madness*

The Plough Inn, Clifton
Hampden, Oxon, has an ancient
crutched foundation.

The Old Albion, Crantock,
Cornwall, is four hundred years
old.

within God's house and to defile it with
scandalous games and lewd discourse . . . '

A century after the Norman invasion, during
the Plantagenet rule of Henry II the first
national tax on ale was levied. A year later
in 1189 the City Council of London, in
common with other local governments of the
day, made a ruling *'that all ale-houses be*
forbidden except those which shall be licensed
by the Common Council of the City at
Guildhall, excepting those belonging to persons
who build of stone, that the city may be secure'.

Throughout the Middle Ages it was the
Church that provided for the needs of
travellers, both temporal and spiritual.
Although guests were not expected to pay
for a night's lodging, it was considered
reasonable that those who could afford to
make a contribution should so do. The
parsimonious King John spent some time at
Bury St. Edmunds and the prior gloomily
wrote in his journal, *'He availed himself of*
the hospitality of St. Edmunds which was
attended with enormous expense, and upon
his departure bestowed nothing upon the Saint,
save thirteen pence sterling which he offered at
Mass'.

As travel increased throughout the realm
it became exceedingly difficult for even the
larger religious establishments to cater for
the many guests requesting accommodation
and food. The responsibility was gradually
transferred to commercially operated
hostelries, although this did not mean that
the monasteries were relinquished from the
responsibility of brewing.

Rose & Crown,
Stratford-upon-Avon, Warws.

The Old Wellington Inn,
Manchester, Lancs.
This inn is one of the oldest
surviving buildings in the city.

The despotic reign of King John had been
curtailed in 1215 by the signing of the
Magna Carta and England was able to settle
down to relative peace and tranquillity on the
home front. The first major act of parliament
affecting the trade of ale was legislated in
1267 by Henry III and became known as
the Assize of Bread and Ale which was to
result in the prices of these two essential
commodities being controlled for the next
three hundred years. A proclamation to the
City of Bristol stated:

*'It is forbidden by the King's writ that any
brewer in the town of Bristol or in the suburbs
of the same town, or any other vending ale
there or elsewhere in the Kingdom of England,
shall sell a gallon of the better ale for more
than three halfpence, and of the weaker ale for
a penny'.*

The document went on to say that anyone
who was indicted for an offence would be
severely punished. An additional act of 1285
to regulate the prices of wines threatened,
*' . . . and if the taverners exceed, their doors
shall be shut'.*

The inns of Chaucer's time were far from
luxurious and many of the pilgrims
journeying to either Canterbury or
Walsingham had to spend the night packed
into large dormitories. Other wayfarers who
were perhaps of more lowly station were
accommodated in the guest houses of some
of the monasteries. The worldly monks were
able to live a life of ease and sauntering
comfort, occasionally giving alms to the poor
and showing lavish hospitality towards
those who could afford to dine at the
Abbot's table.

The New Inn at Gloucester, built in 1457, is typical of many medieval inns to be found up and down the country. It was originally built as a pilgrims' hostel for those visiting the nearby shrine of Edward II who was brutally murdered at Berkeley Castle in 1327.

An inn that one immediately associates with the Crusades must be the Ye Olde Trip to Jerusalem, sheltered beneath the rock on which Nottingham Castle stands. It has brewed its own beer for centuries and is one of a number of inns claiming to be the oldest in the country.

Other possible candidates for this honour include Grantham's Angel & Royal where Richard III signed the death warrant of the Duke of Buckingham in 1493. Masonry in the cellar dates back to 1213, but the main structure is circa 1450.

Meanwhile, back at the inn, many of the supposed pilgrims were able to satisfy their temporal lusts in debauchery and the singing of obscene songs, although the Canterbury publicans were instructed only to admit *'such as be of good disposition and conversation'*.

The taverns certainly were hotbeds of mischief and the weary traveller would often find himself surrounded by a host of thieves and scoundrels eager to rob him of whatever valuables he possessed. The inn, being the natural focal point of the community, attracted a cross section of society and it would have been possible to find a variety of fascinating people, minstrels, troubadours, sorcerers, gamblers, prostitutes and fraudulent rogues. Frequently the innkeepers were in league with robbers and after tipping them off about a likely victim, would expect to have a share of the takings.

The larger inns situated on important routes not only provided the traveller with food and rest but also stabling for horses. You could also expect to find a blacksmith in the vicinity, busily engaged at his forge.

In 1559, the young Queen Elizabeth is reported to have complained about the quality and price of beer. *'A kind of very strong bere calling the same doble-doble-bere which they do commonly utter and sell at a very grate and excessive pryce'*. She ordered that brewers must brew an equal amount of single beer and charge reasonable prices.

During one of the Queen's periodic country tours, one of many she was to make throughout her long reign, the Duke of Leicester wrote to her Lord High Treasurer,

Another ancient inn, The Fighting Cocks at St. Albans is an unusual octagonally-shaped building believed to date back to about 795 when it was built as a boat house to the ancient monastery. An underground passage once connected the inn to the monastery. Oliver Cromwell is said to have stayed there during the Civil War.

The Hoy and Helmet, South Benfleet, Essex.
A hoy was an East Anglian cargo sailing boat, named after its inventor. The helmet may refer to soldiers who were carried in such vessels during the Napoleonic Wars.

Burghley, and criticized the fact that *'There is not one drop of good drink here for her. We were fain to send to London and Kenilworth and divers other places where ale was; her own beer was so strong and there was no man able to drink it'*.

It hardly comes as a surprise to find that a number of our more senior inns played host to the first Queen Elizabeth at some time or another. It is quite possible that a few of the ascribed inns can be authenticated although it is certain that an equal number of claims are spurious.

The **King's Head** at Chigwell, Essex is a striking timbered coaching house, said to have been built during the reign of Henry VIII and it is believed that the Virgin Queen spent a night here during a hunting excursion. Legend said that an unfortunate page boy had his ears cuffed by Her Majesty for *'neglecting his duty'*.

Elizabethan England was truly a 'Golden Age'. The population of England and Wales numbered about 4,000,000, of whom four-fifths lived in rural parts. A census carried out in 1557 showed that there were 14,202 alehouses, 1,631 inns and 329 taverns in England and Wales and the number of licenses issued totalled 19,759.

A price list taken from Castle Combe in Wiltshire for that year indicates that there were at least three different types of ale available and the ale which had matured longer was the most expensive.

Best ale	per gallon	3d
Stale	,, ,,	4d
Second ale	,, ,,	$1\frac{1}{2}$d

This inn, The Sir John Barleycorn, near Ringwood in the New Forest, is named after a reputedly real person who, from time to time, has appeared in literature and has also been associated with beer and brewing.

Another New Forest pub, the Cat & Fiddle at Hinton Admiral has been named after the popular nursery rhyme.

The Talbot, Ledbury, Herefs. possesses a beautiful panelled room which dates from 1596.

| Stale | ,, | ,, | 2d |
| Smallest ale | ,, | ,, | ½d |

Important towns like Reading could boast of as many as 3 taverns, 70 alehouses and 13 inns.

The Elizabethans were free from medieval superstition and expressed their enlightened love of life through music, wit and literature. Shakespeare was undoubtedly a frequent inhabitor of various inns and alehouses up and down the country. He must have certainly been known in the **Falcon,** just opposite where his house, New Place, stood in Stratford-upon-Avon. The Falcon has remained almost unchanged since then but it is not only in Stratford that we find Shakespearean links. He must have often crossed the Clopton Bridge to make the long and tiring journey south towards London.

Most of the taverns en route would have been familiar to him and in London he must have found time to visit many of the notable establishments of the day. The **Mermaid Tavern** which formerly stood in Cheapside was founded in 1603 by Ben Jonson and it is known that Shakespeare used to meet Jonson there. A bankside inn called the **Anchor** was close to the Globe Theatre and perhaps after an exasperating day of rehearsals Shakespeare might have been heard borrowing a line from one of his characters, Christopher Sly in the *Taming of the Shrew 'For God's sake, a pot of small ale'.*

The control and licensing of public houses during the 16th century was the responsibility of the local Justices of the Peace who were selected as residents of high standing and

The Falcon, Stratford-upon-Avon, Warws.

As is to be expected, Stratford-upon-Avon has a number of inns sharing associations with the great bard. There is the White Swan and the Shakespeare Hotel with rooms named after his plays.

The historic Shakespeare Hotel in Chapel Street, adjoining New Place.

endowed with considerable judicial and administrative powers by the monarch. The Church was still an important institution and was reluctant to relinquish any of its powers, particularly where the drinking habits of the local populace were concerned. Church wardens were empowered to break into inns and interrupt the inhabitants, forcibly carrying them off to church if the question of sabbath day observance was involved.

Not that the Church was beyond reproach. The selling of church ales had long been a lucrative source of extra income and Philip Stubbs, writing in his *Anatomie of Abuses* 1585 mentioned: *'The Churche Wardens . . . of every parishe, with the consent of the whole parishe, provide halfe a score or twentie quarters of mault, . . . which mault beeying made into very strong ale or beere, is sette to sale, either in the churche or some other place assigned to that purpose'.* He went on to say how they amused themselves, *'swillying and gullyng night and day, til they be as dronke as rattes, and as blockishe as beastes'.* It was not until 1595 that the selling of church ales was finally prohibited in a decree signed by the Lord Chief Justice in Bridgwater.

Harrison's *Description of England,* 1577 has left us an interesting contemporary account concerning Elizabethan inns.
'Those towns . . . have great and sumptuous innes builded in them, for the receiving of such travellers and strangers as passe to and fro. . . . Every man may use his inne as his owne house . . . and have for his monie how grate or varietie of vittels, and what other service himselfe shall think expedient to call for. Our

The 16th century Feathers Hotel,
Ludlow, Salop.
　　The iron-studded door
shows the arms of a number of
notable families.

Ye Olde Anchor Inn,
Upton-on-Severn, Worcs., is an
early 17th Century timber-framed
hostelry.

*innes are also very well furnished with
naperie, bedding, and tapisterie . . . for all
beside the linnen used at the tables, which is
commonlie washed dailie, is such and so much
as belongeth unto the estate of the ghest. Ech
comer is sure to lie in cleane sheets, wherein
no man hath beene lodged since they came from
the landress . . . '*

It all sounded extremely efficient and
comfortable. The integrity of the landlord
was also stressed and the guest assured that,
*'If he loose oughts whilest he abidest in the
inne, the host is bound by a generall custome
to restore the damage, so that there is no
greater securitie anie where for travellers than
in the greatest innes of England'.* However,
this was not always the case and it was
quite possible for the innkeeper to be in
league with a highwayman, as even Harrison
had warned, *'Certes, I believe not that chapman
or traveller in England is robbed by the waie
without the knowledge of some of them; for when
he cometh into the inne and alighteth from his
horse, the hostler forthwith is verie busy to take
down his budget or capcase . . . which he peiseth
slilie in his hand to feel the weight thereof'.*

Obviously the innkeeper would ensure that
the reputation of the inn was not tarnished
and that outrages were not to be carried out
on the premises. Certainly the Queen's
Highway was not a safe place for the
unprotected traveller, as is seen from many
contemporary accounts. It is probable that
Shakespeare was the victim of a highwayman
on at least one occasion. Shakespeare himself
referred to the seamy side of inn life when
he wrote about the inn-yard at Rochester in
King Henry IV.

The picturesque New Inn at
Clovelly, Devon.

The Bear Inn, Woodstock, Oxon,
is believed to date back to 1237.
Much of the present structure is
16th century.

Hopcroft's Holt at Steeple Ashton, Oxfordshire is associated with the notorious highwayman Claude Duval, who, on one occasion is said to have robbed a couple of £400. Having the audacity to ask the lady to dance with him, he refunded £300 when she accepted his invitation. Duval was hanged in 1670 and when, several years later, the landlord and his wife were found mysteriously murdered it was said that his ghost had returned.

In many places the accommodation that inns offered was almost as primitive and unsavoury as the homes of the poor but they were always important social and cultural centres, providing relaxation and refreshment to a cross section of the population.

Many of the wealthy inhabitants would adjourn to the local tavern with their guests, where a greater selection of wines was often available than could be found in their own cellars.

Not only did the menfolk spend an evening enjoying themselves at the local tavern. There would be such amusements as eating, drinking, fiddling and drama and the perceptive Thomas Platter in *Travels in England* 1599 was able to observe: '*And what is particularly curious is that the women as well as the men, in fact more often than they, will frequent the taverns and ale-houses for enjoyment. They count it a great honour to be taken there and given wine with sugar to drink; and if only one woman is invited, then she will bring three or four other women along and they gaily toast each other; the*

In the Market Place at Bungay, Suffolk, stands the Three Tuns, and on the opposite side of the road, the King's Head.

The London Apprentice, Isleworth, Middlesex, near the quiet historic quay, is a popular resting place for tourists. It is said to have received its name from the apprentices of the Livery companies who used to row up river.

The Rising Sun, Coltishall, on the Norfolk Broads.

*husband afterwards thanks him who has given
his wife such pleasure, for they deem it a real
kindness'.*

It all sounded jolly good fun and presumably
everyone was able to leave as the best of
friends. Gallants who spent enjoyable
evenings at taverns would often hire guides
to carry ladies home with lanterns.

Perhaps it would be fitting to let Fynes
Moryson sum up the character of the
Elizabethan inn, as he wrote in his *Itinerary
1617.*

*'The world affords not such innes as England
hath, either for food and cheape entertainment
after the guests' owne pleasure, or for humble
attandance on passengers, yea, even in very
poor villages. For as soon as a passenger
comes to an inne, the servants run to him, and
one takes his horse, and walks him till he be
cold, then rubs him and gives him meate. . . .
Another servant gives the passenger his private
chamber, and kindles his fire: the third puls
off his boots and makes them cleane. . . . And
when he sits down at table, the host or hostess
will accompany him or if they have many
guests will at least visit him, taking it for
courtesy to be bid sit down. While he eats, if
he have company especially, he shall be
offered music, which he may freely take or
refuse. . . . A man cannot more freely
command in his own house than he may do in
his inne. And at parting, if he give some few
pence to the chamberlain and ostler, they wish
him a happy journey'.*

An early edict produced during the reign of
James I laid down specific rules and
regulations concerning the general
administration and running of inns, to be

The Old Welsh Harp at Waltham Abbey, Essex. The adjoining house was originally a brew-house and the pub probably takes its name from the harp-shaped reservoir which is in the vicinity.

The Laurel Inn is at Robin Hood's Bay on the Yorkshire coast.

observed by both innkeepers and guests alike. Solemnly it quoted various scriptural references that pertained to inns and ended by adjuring the guest to *'Eat and drinke for necessity and strength, and not for lust'*.

In 1606 a new act was passed, placing further restrictions upon the buying and selling of ale and beer. The Repression of Drunkenness Act replaced earlier laws and felt that it needed to be explicit by saying: *'The ancient and principal true use of innes and victuallinge houses was for the receipte, relief and lodginge of wayfaring people travelling from place to place'*.

A 'wayfaring' person later became known as the 'bona fide' traveller and was permitted to obtain drinks at hours that were normally forbidden to local residents. This often resulted in hilariously amusing mass exoduses from one town to another so that the residents from one town could be found drinking in the neighbouring town, thus evading the licensing laws.

Although parliamentary acts generally tend to be unpopular when they are designed to curb social and drinking activities and it is possible that the dour monarch disapproved of drink as much as he disliked tobacco, the law did provide certain safeguards that were in the traveller's favour. Ale-house keepers were required to keep 'one or more spare beds' for the lodging of strangers and a landlord who refused to furnish a room without good cause could be compelled to accept the guest, with the help of the local constable. Constables were authorised to force admittance into any inn.

The White Horse, Chilgrove,
Sussex.

The Montagu Arms, Beaulieu,
Hants., shows the arms of the
Montagu family.

It was only the tavern keepers who were exempt from this law and were forbidden to provide lodgings. One unfortunate publican in Hitchin was charged with the offence of *'exposing bread and beer as well for men and horses'*. (Hertfordshire County Records, Vol I: page 30). The Stuarts were, in time, to pass many more acts, none of which were popular with the brewers who had to face increased taxation. Charles I granted a special charter to the citizens of London enabling them to construct signs for the purpose of *'the better finding out such citizen's dwellings'* and also served as address locaters long before the idea of street numbering was thought of. As early as 1393 Richard II had ordered publicans to display signs.

One of the most elaborate and unusual inn signs ever to be built, either then or today, was at Scole in Norfolk and belonged to the **White Hart Inn**. It consisted of a huge carved archway, decorated with an array of Biblical and legendary characters and animals. An engraving of this sign can be seen at the Norwich Central Library. The actual sign was destroyed almost two hundred years ago.

Because so many inns and taverns were situated close to churches, and in some cases actually within churchyards, church wardens and choirboys were frequently seen slipping into the inn whilst the sermon was being preached. This was confirmed by Defoe in the lines:

'Wherever God erects a House of Prayer,
The Devil's sure to build a chapel there,
And 'twill be found upon examination,
The latter has the larger congregation'.

The George, Crawley, Sussex. Situated on the Brighton road, this former medieval dwelling is believed to have become an inn in 1615. It was a popular stage-coach halt and the distinctive gallows sign has been a feature of the inn for well over two hundred and fifty years.

The Prince of Wales, Ledbury, Herefs., in the delightful cobbled Church Lane is one of many beautiful timbered buildings.

It was during the 17th century that we see
the beginning of many of today's leading
brewing companies. Most larger towns had
their own breweries and it is interesting to
note that during Cromwell's short austere
regime he was nicknamed 'The Brewer',
after his mother who had been a brewster in
Huntingdon. It is believed that he first
plotted to overthrow the King at the **Bear**
in Cambridge.

Truman's had been established since 1666.
John Courage began in Southwark in 1787 by
purchasing the Horsely Down brewery;
Southwark ale was known during the 14th
century. Ralph Thrale also had a brewery there
on the site of the former Globe Theatre. This
was later bought by Robert Barclay and
John Perkins and subsequently became part
of the Courage group.

The history of brewers tends to be obscured by
the fact that businesses changed hands and
names were frequently altered. The subject is
worthy of further investigation. Simond's of
Reading and George's of Bristol were taken
over by Courage in 1785 and 1788. Samuel
Whitbread had established his brewery in
London's Chiswell Street and Watney's were
brewing at Wimbledon. Other names rooted in
the 17th and 18th centuries included Allsopp,
Combe, Charrington, Bass, Worthington,
Tetley and Guinness.

The streets of 17th century London must have
created quite a visual impact on any visitor,
who, for the first time, saw a multitude of
elaborate towering signs. Thomas Heywood,
author of the amusing *Roxburghe Ballads*
parodied the names and the types of individuals
who frequented the various taverns:

The King's Head, Lymington, Hants., stands in a charming Georgian cobbled street.

The George, Stamford, Lincs. This well-known hotel has the largest surviving gallows sign.

'The Gentrie went to the King's Head,
The Nobles unto the Crowne,
The Knights went unto the Golden Fleece,
And the Ploughmen to the Clowne.

The Clergie will dine at the Miter,
The Vintners at the Three Tuns,
The Userers to the Devil will goe,
And the Fryers to the Nunnes.

The Cheter will dine at the Checker,
The Picke-pockets in a blind alehouse,
Til on they tride then up Holborne they ride,
And they there end up at the Gallowes'.

The great London fire of 1666 wiped out most
of the street signs, as well as entirely
destroying a large part of the city. In 1667 an
act was passed which prohibited large
overhanging street signs. By the turn of the
century, this statute had been disregarded and
many unwieldy signs re-appeared in the
London streets. It was not until four people
were killed in a street tragedy in 1718 that
further action was taken. The accident
occurred in Bride Street when a large
overhead sign crashed down, bringing with it
the entire front of a shop. There were still
those willing to flout the law and as late as
1787, the biographer of Joseph Hanway wrote:
'How comfortless must be the sensations of an
elderly female stopped in the street on a windy
day under a large old sign loaded with lead and
iron in full swing over her head, and perhaps a
torrent of dirty water falling near from a
projecting spout, ornamented with the mouth
and teeth of a dragon. These dangers and
distresses are now at an end; and we may think
of them as the sailor does of a storm that has
subsided . . .'
In 1711 Joseph Addison, co-founder of the

The Rising Sun, Lynmouth,
Devon, forms part of a lovely
terrace of historic thatched
cottages.

Journey's End Inn, Ringmore,
Devon, claims to date from the
12th century.

The New Inn, Winchelsea, Sussex,
forms part of an attractive
Regency terrace.

Spectator had observed: *'Our streets are filled with Blue Boars, Black Swans and Red Lions, not to mention Flying Pigs and Hogs in Armour, with many other creatures more extraordinary than any in the deserts of Africa . . . One famous sign, hanging outside a public house in Drury Lane, was of so striking a nature that every day crowds of country people could be seen assembled there, vacantly staring at it for hours. It consisted of a full-length picture of Shakespeare . . . suspended in an elaborate carved and gilded frame from some rich ironwork'*. That particular sign remained until 1775 and could be seen after in a pawnbroker's shop window, until it rotted away.

Much has been written about the 'Gin Era' between 1720 and 1750, when cheap gin was generally available. This was attributed to the fact that between 1740 and 1742 there were twice as many burials as baptisms. *'Drunk for 1d, dead drunk for 2d, straw for nothing'* so a popular saying went. Hogarth's propagandist cartoons, *Gin Lane* and the *Four Stages of Cruelty* depicted drunken debauchery of the most evil kind, whereas the contrasting peace and tranquillity of *Beer Street* is distinctly noticeable.

One of the greatest pub-crawlers of the time was the burly lexicographer and prominent literary figure, Dr. Samuel Johnson. The faithful biographer, Boswell, recorded his friend as saying: *'There is nothing which has yet been contrived by man, by which so much happiness is produced as by a good tavern or inn'*. Johnson spent many an hour in various London pubs and the **Cheshire Cheese** in Johnson Court, today exhibits his notorious chair. Perhaps, above all other taverns, it is the

The Red Lion, Northleach, Glos.,
in an historic old wool town set
in the Cotswolds.

Bel & the Dragon, Cookham,
Berks, recalls an old legend.

Mitre in Fleet Street which we mostly associate with Johnson, although this should not be confused with the **Mitre** that Shakespeare knew.

The scholarly Mrs. Thrale, daughter-in-law to the brewer, was a close friend of Johnson's and it is probable that he would have been acquainted with the processes of brewing after visiting the Southwark brewery.

Ownership of many of the taverns and pubs was already in the hands of several of the breweries. An advertisement in the *Daily Courant* emphasised the advantages of free houses over those that were tied:
'A handsome corner public house, in New Belton Street, St. Giles' . . . just empty, well situated and free from bondage of any particular brewer'.

During the years 1751-53 further laws were enacted, this time to prevent distillers from selling or retailing spirits in unlicensed premises. Annual licenses were made statutory and anyone who wished to apply for a license for the first time was required to produce character certificates from clergymen.

The 1751 act preambled:
'Whereas the immoderate drinking of distilled spiritous liquors by persons of the meanest and lowest sort, hath of late years increased, to the great detriment of the health and morals of the common people . . .'

The coaching inns played an essential part in 18th century travel and, generally speaking, the service that they provided was good.

Regular scheduled coach services stopped at selected inns along the route where the horses would be changed and passengers could rest

The Mermaid Inn, Rye, Sussex. This well preserved inn was a notorious haunt of smugglers during the 18th century, and was awarded the Queen's Award to Industry in 1973, in recognition of its achievements in attracting overseas visitors.

Bobby's, Edinburgh.

and take refreshments. Most important towns were well served, with several coaches arriving and leaving every day. Bath, the fashionable society resort presided over by Beau Nash was particularly well provided with coaches.

Travellers were still not infrequently stopped and robbed during a journey and despite the certain fate that befell a captured highwayman, there were plenty of rogues who anxiously engaged in robbing whoever they chanced to meet. The writings of Horace Walpole and the poem by Alfred Noyes have helped to evoke a romantic glamour around the exploits of highwaymen. There was still a persistent belief that many innkeepers were in league with the villains. In 1876 some workmen who were demolishing an inn near Selby stumbled across the remains of a body with a mail bag, hidden in a secret alcove.

Richard Turpin, alias John Palmer is alleged to have killed his friend Tom King in the yard of the **Red Lion** in Whitechapel High Street, a short while before he was hanged at York. Others met their fate at Tyburn (where London's Marble Arch now stands). It was customary to allow the condemned prisoners to have a drink before being executed and the carts would often stop between the prison and the gallows. Swift wrote:

'As clever Tom Clinch, while the rabble was bawling,
Rode stately through Holborn to die in his calling,
He stopped at the George for a bottle of sack,
And promised to pay for it – when he came back!'

Throughout the 19th century, acts of parliament affecting licensing, opening hours and other measures aimed at curbing drunkenness considerably changed the role of

38

The Smith's Arms, Godmanstone, Dorset, is the smallest public house in the United Kingdom, measuring just 10 feet wide and 4 feet high at the eaves. It was personally licensed by Charles II who stopped to have his horse shod. When he demanded a drink, the blacksmith told him that he was not licensed to sell ale. The King immediately granted a license in order to get a drink. The bar, however, is not the smallest to be found in the UK.

The Three Mariners in Scarborough dates back to 1300 and was for many years a favourite haunt of smugglers. The building contains several secret escape passages and although no longer used as a pub, it has been specially preserved as a museum. The bar contains a snug which is a common feature of many of our older pubs. They were intended as intimate, exclusive compartments said to 'protect the social susceptibilities of drinkers'.

the pub. More and more pubs became tied to brewers who claimed that they could build better premises and provide a greater selection of drinks.

During Wellington's time as Prime Minister, *The Beer House Act* came into force, entitling anyone to retail beer in return for an annual fee of two guineas. The result of this was quite phenomenal, with 30,978 new beer houses being opened. Understandably, many publicans objected to the competition and suggested that the nation would derive more by appropriating church property, in preference to property belonging to licensed victuallers. It was argued that the clergy did not attend to the poor whereas the pubs did!

The artistic and literary works of the last century have left a rich variety of pub descriptions but the name that most people associate with pubs, is of course, Dickens. The **Ye Olde King's Head** at Chigwell became the *Maypole* in *Barnaby Rudge*. The **Leather Bottle** at Chobham (Kent) contains several mementos of Dickens and any readers of the *Pickwick Papers* will no doubt remember the *Bull* at Rochester or the *Great White Horse* at Ipswich, where Pickwick mistook a lady's bedroom for his own. There are also a number of Dickensian pubs taking their names from famous characters, such as the old **Our Mutual Friend** in Stevenage which stood close to Knebworth House, where Dickens occasionally visited his friend Bulwer Lytton.

There are numerous other literary associations with various pubs but perhaps one of the most amusing is the **Swan** in Grasmere. Sir Walter Scott was staying with the penurious William Wordsworth, and, preferring the hospitality

The Axe & Compass, Hemingford
Abbots, Hunts.

The Pilot Boat Inn, Bembridge,
Isle of Wight.
This unusual-looking inn was
originally a cottage but it has
subsequently been licensed and
rebuilt to give it a nautical
atmosphere.

The Pike & Eel Inn, near
Needingworth, Hunts.

of the local, used regularly to slip out of the house. One day the two men called at the inn to hire some ponies when the landlord tactlessly remarked that Scott had arrived a little early for his daily tot!

William Makepeace Thackeray couldn't help writing a verse about a particular barmaid to whom he was attracted, named Peggy:
'See her as she moves,
Scarce the ground she touches,
Airy as a fay,
Graceful as a duchess . . .'

The Victorians built hundreds of public houses and although many of them were hardly an architectural asset, there were 118,602 licensed premises in 1869 and almost 50,000 breweries and distilleries. Since then there has been a drastic reduction and today there are just over 73,000 premises in the United Kingdom.

Of the 95 brewers, 7 comprise national companies and there are about 15,000 free houses.

The swing towards temperance at the end of the last century presented a serious threat to the industry and it was partly to offset this that the Brewers' Society was established in 1904. The distillers also formed their own society. New laws concerning Sunday closing came into effect but in Wales, some astute publicans provided their customers with specially made metal flasks which could be concealed beneath clothing. These 'belly cans' made it possible for customers to take drinks home on Sundays.

Several temperance societies were formed, with the support of most of the religious institutions. Young children were

The Sole Bay Inn, Southwold,
Suffolk, is a quayside pub,
overshadowed by a lighthouse.

The Cob Tree , Ightham , Kent.

indoctrinated into signing pledges of abstinence at ages when they would never have even contemplated taking liquor.

Probably the most serious threat to the trade came in 1915 when the *Defence of the Realm Act* nationalised 321 licensed premises in the Carlisle, Gretna and Cromarty areas which also included two breweries. These areas were important war production zones and it was felt that essential work was being hampered by excessive drinking. Since 1970, they have been returned to private ownership.

In 1923 drinking was made illegal for those under the age of 18. Throughout the 20's and 30's various attempts to introduce prohibition failed, despite considerable pressure from a number of distinguished people.

The pub has managed to survive in a world of radical change even although television and other forms of relaxation have produced competition. Over a period of hundreds of years, the pub has attained stature and maturity and today has finally become respected and appreciated as an important community social centre.

The George, Chepstow, Mon.,
stands beside the old town gate.

The Fox and Hounds, Barley, Herts.

Pub Signs

In bygone days the pictorial sign was used as a means of identification which could be recognised by even the most ignorant. Long before street naming and numbering became fashionable, the sign was an essential means of locating addresses. Some of the earliest signs were used by the Romans. A chequered sign has been found in the ruins of Pompeii and the ale stake and evergreen is one of the earliest signs used to denote an inn.

Later, other objects, some of them associated with brewing, became synonymous with ale-houses and taverns. Because the Church was closely tied to many of the early inns, the signs appropriately showed a religious influence of apostles, saints and crusades. Other signs reflected royal and heraldic influences.

A certain amount of prestige was attached to establishments which could display the most original and colourful signs and in many instances the work was done by accomplished artists of the day. The less inspired signmaker could always revert to one of the many hackneyed rhymes in an effort to tempt custom:

'If you go by and thirsty be,
The fault's on you and not on me.
Fixed here I am, and hinder none,
So refresh, and pay, and travel on.'

and for the fatigued coach traveller or rider:–

'In this tavern you may find
Everything to suit your mind,
Good wine, good fish, and flesh in courses
Coaches, chaises, harness, horses'.

Often a pub name can mean a lot more than it superficially suggests. Usually the names have

Religious Signs

been carefully chosen, representing a rich
accumulation of local folklore and history.
Sign spotters can find an extensive variety of
artistically attractive notices, although there
are also, of course, a few shoddy and inferior
ones to be seen.

Religious Signs

Some of the earliest religious signs are strongly
linked with the Crusades. The **Ye Olde Trip to
Jerusalem** at Nottingham is an obvious
example, as are names like the **Turk's** or
Saracen's Head. There is a well known
Saracen's Head at Ware, in Hertfordshire.
Devils and demons make interesting subjects.
There used to be a well known **Devil** near St.
Dunstan's Church, London and the sign
depicted St. Dunstan pulling the devil by his
nose. Perhaps one of the most enigmatic
subjects are our first parents, Adam and Eve,
who can leave the artist with a great deal of
scope for his imagination. The inevitable
happened in one village where the
unfortunate artist had the sign returned to
him with instructions to equip the duo with
fig leaves. Later still, the sign was again
returned following complaints about the
artist's interpretation of the serpent.
The **Lion & Lamb** depicts the sacrificial Christ
and Peter likened 'Satan unto a lion'. **Cross
Keys** are associated with the apostle Peter.
The **Goat & Compasses** is believed by many to
be a corruption of a Puritan motto 'God

47

encompasses us'. Most *New Inn* signs are in fact
old establishments and can be classified as
religious in origin, taking their names from the
days when inns were administered by
monasteries. The **New Inn** of Gloucester is a
good example of a pilgrims' hostelry. The
Mitre is a well known ecclesiastical symbol and
several pubs bearing the name were known to
Shakespeare, Jonson and Johnson. Some
religious signs disappeared after the
Reformation and it is said that 'papistical'
signs such as the **Nuns** were changed to **Angels.**
Some Angel signs depict Michael the Archangel
carrying a sword and shield.

Various saints appear on signs but one of the
most common is England's patron saint,
George, killing the dragon. Both characters
may also appear on boards separately and a
number of George's were changed to represent
reigning monarchs. Various **Bell** and **Anchor**
compositions are used. Paul described hope as
the 'anchor of the soul', hence the variation
Hope and Anchor.

Heraldic and Emblematic Signs

A wide selection of differing signs within this
grouping represent the monarchy and
aristocracy. During the Middle Ages it was
customary for the houses of the nobility to be
used as hostelries, when the families were
absent. The houses displayed the family's
heraldic coats of arms. Many a shrewd
innkeeper showed his loyalty by adopting the

heraldic device of a neighbouring noble or of
the monarch. These signs must have changed
as frequently as heads rolled and when
Richard III was killed many of the Plantagenet
White Boars were subsequently painted blue
to represent the Earl of Oxford who was
instrumental in placing Henry Tudor on
the throne. Shortly before being killed, Richard
spent his last night in the **White Boar** at
Leicester.

Signs depicting animals and birds are also
often associated with noble families. The
Greyhound is the emblem of the Tudors,
although it may since have become more
associated with sport. The **Talbot,** an extinct
breed of dog, represents the Earls of
Shrewsbury. A more vulgar form has been
passed down as the **Spotted Dog.** Swans appear
in the arms of the Buckinghams. The **Swan** at
Denham, Bucks shows an example of a chained
swan.

One of the Warwicks is reputed to have fought
with a bear, a symbol which the family later
adopted. This may also appear as a sign which
formerly was used to advertise bear baiting.
The Stanleys, Earls of Derby, have adopted an
unusual emblem, the **Eagle and Child,** and are
said to have taken it from the Latham family
of Lancashire, to whom Sir John Stanley was
related by marriage. One of the Lathams was
rumoured to have adopted a child found in an
eagle's nest in Ireland. There are numerous
rose signs representing the houses of York and
Lancaster. The **Rose Revived** and the **Rose &
Crown** commemorate the end of the wars
between the two houses. Property which
stood on ground once owned by the sovereign
was often given the name **Crown. Three**

Heraldic and Emblematic Signs .

Crowns refers to the Magi – the three Kings of Orient. The **Crown & Cushion** at Minley, Hampshire has a yew tree, trimmed to the shape of a crown resting on a cushion to commemorate the arrest of Colonel Blood at the inn.

Lions are also popular symbols and appear as **Red Lions, Golden Lions, Black Lions, White Lions** and occasionally, **Blue Lions.** The **Red Lion** represented John of Gaunt and is also found in the arms of Scotland. **Golden Lions** are emblems of England. **White Lions** belong to the Dukes of Norfolk.

Tabards are short sleeved heraldic tunics, blazoned with the arms of the sovereign. Our illustration shows an unusual and realistic carved sign of the **Tabard.**

When Charles II escaped following the Battle of Worcester, he is said to have hidden in an oak tree at Boscobel, hence the popularity of the **Royal Oak** sign.

Many of our monarchs appear on signs, either above the sovereign's name or as the **King's** or **Queen's Head.** Occasionally a playing card representation is used.

The **White Hart,** depicting a pure white stag wearing a gold collar and chain can be traced back to the story told by Pliny in which Alexander the Great captured a stag, placing a gold collar around its neck. Richard II adopted the emblem. Throughout the country there are numerous signs depicting the coats of arms of local noble families. The **Fleur De Lys** obviously relates to the Conquest and shows a Norman warrior.

Travel Signs

Transport through the ages is a subject well covered by inn signs. Ever since the Romans set up shop here, roadside inns have provided refreshments and rest for travellers. Our signs depict various travel scenes, ranging from the primitive to the highly sophisticated modes of transport. The **Pilgrim** and the **Traveller's Rest** are often seen. This sign shows a Roman Centurion. There is an unusual sign in Mayfair, London showing a foot-post man delivering mail. The pub is called **I am the only Running Footman.** The stage coach features on many signs and names like the **Coach and Horses,** the **Dairy Maid** and the **Toll House** are quite common. A famous coach, the **Gloucester Flying Machine** can be seen at Brockworth, Gloucestershire. The **Horse and Groom** is another popular sign, and was used to advertise stabling facilities. Horseshoes and blacksmiths were also used for this purpose.

The industrial revolution saw the demise of horse travel and the gradual introduction of steam railways. The **Railway King** at York shows the portrait of George Hudson, a pioneer builder. Many of the great railway hotels and inns no longer survive and some of the existing places have changed their names. It is, however, still possible to find such names as **Great Northern, Great Western, North British, Iron Horse, Puffing Billy, Rocket, Deltic** and the **Railway Tavern.** A model of Stephenson's *Rocket* is affixed to the structure of the **Iron Horse** at Newton Aycliffe, Co. Durham.

Nautical scenes have fared better and it is easy enough to find a variety of ships, either old or new. The **Anchor** is sometimes used to denote a religious meaning but there are plenty of

Sporting Signs

Jolly Sailors, **Admirals** and **Ships**. Battles and events are also popular, with names like the **Admiral Benbow** and **Trafalgar Tavern**.

Names like the **Airman** can be found in the vicinity of several airports. At Feltham, Middlesex, a sign shows an airman standing in the foreground with a Red Arrows' display in the sky. In Hatfield, Hertfordshire, near where De Haviland's developed the Comet stands a pub of the same name. Just outside Gloucester stands a pub which bears the name the **Jet and Whittle** alluding to the nearby factory whence the first jet engine flight took place in 1941.

A pub in Hastings, instead of showing the Iron Duke, displays **Wellington** bombers.

Cars have not been excluded – the **Silver Ghost** at Alvaston, Derby shows a Rolls-Royce on one side and on the reverse the more usual interpretation. The **Flying Lady** at Hungerford, Berkshire also shows a Rolls-Royce car.

Sporting Signs

Most sporting activities have appeared on signs and their meanings are self explanatory. Cricketers revere the **Bat and Ball** in Hambledon, Berkshire, which celebrates the 18th century captain, John Nyren. One side of the sign shows his portrait whilst the other depicts a game on the green. Nottingham's Trent Bridge ground has the **Test Match** and Lord's has its **Tavern**. W. G. Grace and F. R. Spofforth share the sign at the **Yorker** in

The BAT & BALL
John Nyren of Hambledon
1764–1837

London's Piccadilly. The **Cricketers** at Hebing
End, Hertfordshire shows 18th century period
costumes and bats. A sign at Newbury,
Berkshire is a pun, showing a young girl leaping
over the wicket with the lettering **The Maiden
Over.**

Some of the football clubs have their own pubs
like Arsenal whose supporters can drink at the
Gunners, Finsbury Park. Golfers are not as
well represented although places named after
famous holes can sometimes be seen.

Anglers can drink at the **Pike and Eel**,
Needingworth, Huntingdonshire. Isaac
Walton is celebrated at the **Compleat Angler** at
Marlow, Buckinghamshire and the **Isaac
Walton** at Brimsdown, Middlesex.

Horse Racing has always been a popular
subject and names like the **Horse & Groom** or
Horseshoes can refer to either coaching inns or
racing establishments. The **Derby Arms** at
East Sheen, Surrey shows Sansovino winning
at Epsom in 1924. A St. Leger winner,
Charles XII is shown along with the 1813
Altisidora. The name **Arkle** has become
immortal, as has the **Master Robert** who, as a
racehorse developed bad legs and was relegated
to pulling a milk cart and yet went on to win
the Grand National.

Blood sports have always been common. The
Fighting Cocks at St. Albans reminds us of the
now illegal sport of cock-fighting. Other inns
have had a tradition for bear-baiting. The
Cat and Custard Pot is an unusual sign at
Shipton Moyne, Wiltshire. On one side can be
seen a cat, licking a bowl but the reverse side
shows the literary character Jorrocks at a hunt
meeting. The crafty fox turns up on a number
of signs but perhaps the most extraordinary

The Kill on the Cat & Custard Pot Day

Fox and Hounds is the old gallows sign at Barley, Hertfordshire which completely spans the road. It is said that the name originated after a fox took refuge in a kennel at the back of the inn. Unfortunately, in 1950 the inn was destroyed by fire but the preserved sign was transferred to another pub just a few yards up the road. Hawking and falconry are often shown. Shakespeare knew the **Falcon** at Stratford-upon-Avon. Several monarchs, including Elizabeth I have used the bird as a heraldic symbol.

Signs Depicting People

All kinds of people, whether real life, imaginary or legendary can be seen looking down from their lofty pub signs. Politicians, men of war, royalty, inventive geniuses, noblemen, artists, writers, fictional and folk-lore characters have all been used.

Green Men are traditionally popular inn signs and another green man who allegedly robbed the rich to help the poor called **Robin Hood** is also frequently seen.

Heroic deeds can assure lasting fame and there is certainly no shortage of such people as **Wellington, Nelson, Marquis of Granby, Duke of York** and **Sir Francis Drake.** Politicians and statesmen such as **Oliver Cromwell, Palmerston, Pitt, Gladstone, John F. Kennedy, Churchill, Peel, Disraeli, Lloyd George** and **Clement Attlee.** When Attlee's portrait sign was unveiled for

the pub's opening in Fulham, attended by his son, it was discovered that the artist had depicted the former prime minister wearing a red tie. The sign had to be removed and the colour of the tie changed because, as it was pointed out, he never ever wore a red tie!

Great men like **Wren, Brunel, Cook, Shakespeare** and **Dickens** have all been captured by the signpainter's brush. We also find famous women like **Florence Nightingale, Amy Johnson, Jenny Lind, Nell Gwynne, Emma Hamilton, Nellie Dean, Eliza Doolittle** and the unfortunate **Silent Woman,** showing a headless female. Perhaps the artist decided to make amends when he painted the **Nag's Head** which was not the usual horse portrait.

Regimental orders are found, particularly close to barracks and the signs often depict a regiment's most famous battle scene. Pubs have not been without their share of villainy so it is fitting that we should also come across rogues like **Claude Duval,** the **Wicked Lady,** the **Highwayman** and scenes depicting punishments such as the **Stocks or Gibbet.**

Doctor William Harvey who discovered the principal of blood circulation is shown on a distinctive sign at the **William Harvey** near Ashford, Kent. The pub stands on the former site of the Harvey Cottages at Willesborough and the sign is unusual in that it uses a contemporary engraving of the doctor. One of the most quaint and infrequent signs that we see nowadays is the **Five Alls** showing five representations:– 'I Pray for All', 'I Fight for All', 'I Rule for All', 'I Plead for All', and 'I Work for All'. Other variations of this theme are known to exist.

Legendary characters which include **Dick**

Trade Signs

Whittington, the **Pied Piper,** the **Babes in the Wood, Tom Thumb, Robinson Crusoe, Jack and Jill** and **Mother Hubbard** seem to be very popular. The local conundrum about the polygamous man and his seven wives is depicted on a sign at St. Ives, Huntingdon:

'As I was going to St. Ives
I met a man with seven wives,
Each wife with seven sacks
Each sack with seven cats...'

One of Hogarth's original signs has often been imitated. It is called a **Load of Mischief** and depicts a man carrying on his shoulders, fastened by a chain, his drunken wife, a monkey and a magpie. Another of his signs is slightly more distasteful, showing John the Baptist's head on a charger and entitled **Good Eating.**

Trade Signs

It used to be common practice for all businesses to display descriptive trade signs, but nowadays, with the exception of barbers, chemists and possibly pawnbrokers, it is only the brewing industry which has kept the tradition alive. Varying trades can be found on our pub signs and some of them would indicate an historical association. The smallest pub in Britain, the **Smith's Arms,** Godmanstone, Dorset was a blacksmith's forge in Charles II's day. He stopped there to have his horse shod and when told he couldn't buy

a drink he immediately granted a license and the pub was named the **Smith's Arms.**

Places called the **Farrier's Arms** or the **Three Horseshoes** could well have formerly housed a forge.

The **Wheatsheaf** has links with the Earls of Exeter but is usually associated with baking. Traditional farming implements such as the **Plough,** the **Reaper** and the **Haycart** are frequently seen, as are names like the **Jolly Farmer, Poulterer's Arms, Gardener's Arms** and **Ploughboy.**

Apart from the obvious Biblical associations, **Noah's Ark** has served as the crest of the London Company of Shipwrights. The **Lamb** represented the tailoring trade and the **Lamb & Flag** has been derived from the Merchant Tailors' Company.

The **Ye Olde Pump House** of Hastings is so named because at one time it was the only place where people could draw fresh water in the town. The bar contains an interesting collection of curios and bric-a-brac.

Watermen have the **Watermen's Arms** and in Anglesey, in the town of Llangefni there is a pub in the market square called the **Market Vaults.**

The **Fleece** or **Woolpack** have been used as emblems for the wool trade since the 14th century.

London's Fetter Lane has the **Printer's Devil,** a modern pub rebuilt after the war and containing an interesting collection of printing ephemera. It is hardly surprising to find several signs directly relating to the brewing trade. Tuns are used as the arms of the ancient Company of Vintners and there are plenty of

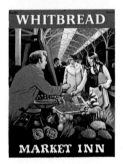

the following names to be found: **Three Tuns, Hoop & Grapes, Vineyard, Bunch of Grapes, Hop Pole,** and the **Barley Mow,** a traditional countryside sign. **Health to the Barley Mow** is a replica of one painted by Hogarth, showing farmworkers celebrating after a successful harvest.

When new public houses are opened, members of the public are often invited to participate in submitting suggestions for names. The **William Cookworthy** at St. Austell, Cornwall was a popular choice, honouring a notable character who was once associated with the local china clay industry.

Animal Signs

Several of the animals that turn up on signs appear as family crests or coats of arms. Sports and hunting pastimes account for many animals like dogs, hares, rabbits, foxes, stags, falcons, eagles and hawks.

Horses have always been popular symbols, particularly **White Horses** which are sometimes associated with the Hanoverian coat of arms. Around Wiltshire and the West Country, a number of **White Horse** signs relate to the chalk figures cut into the downs.

Various birds such as swans, ducks, magpies, doves, pelicans and cocks are fairly common. At Stonham, Suffolk there is an unusual gallows sign at the **Magpie** which spans the road.

Unusual Signs

Various fishes and sea creatures abound, particularly around the coastal towns and villages.

Cats have always been popular, whether they be the pantomime **Puss in Boots, Cheshire Cat, Mad Cat, Rampant Cat** or the musical **Cat & Fiddle.**

Humorous animals such as the **Snooty Fox, Whistling Duck, Dun Cow** and others can usually arouse a smile. The **Pig & Whistle** is an old name thought to be a corruption of Peg and Wassail, a phrase associated with the custom of drinking to pegs.

The village of Lanivet, Cornwall has a rare animal sign – a **Panda.** One of the village's local industries used to be the growing of bamboos which were used to feed the late Chi Chi of London Zoo.

The faithfulness of a dog is remembered in Edinburgh, the home of the famous Greyfriars Bobby who kept vigil for his departed master. A nearby pub has been named **Bobby's.**

Unusual Signs

This last category includes a few of the many unusual and striking pub signs that are either amusing or of a serious nature.

A sign in Chingford shows a side of beef being knighted by King James I and is called the **Sir Loin.** The **World Turned Upside Down,** near Reading shows a donkey sitting in a cart being pulled by a man, a pig killing a butcher,

a bear with a dancing man, a rat chasing a cat and dogs ridden by foxes chasing a man! Knaresborough has the **End of the World**.

The **Hole in the Wall** is an amusing name which is said to have originated from a hole in the wall of a debtor's prison, through which the inmates received gifts. The Highwayman Claude Duval was captured at a pub of the same name in London. The sign in the illustration is a modern interpretation.

The **Snow Drop Inn** of Lewes, Sussex sounds a pretty enough name but it is not named after the flower. An avalanche killed several people in the area during the 19th century.

Another Sussex pub, the **Runt-in-Tun** has just been reopened after a number of years of closure. The ancient name really means pig in the barrel.

The **Nut Shell**, so appropriately named, at Bury St. Edmunds has the smallest bar, measuring a mere fifteen feet.

Dirty Dick's in Bishopsgate, London is named after an old hermit. Architecturally, one of the most exciting modern pubs is an extraordinary 70 foot high fairy-tale castle at Dunstable called the **Windsock**, in honour of the local gliding club.

The **Crooked Billet** sign is made out of wood and contains an unusual inscription which has been copied from the fireplace of the inn. The **Four Counties** Inn happens to stand on No Man's Heath where the counties of Staffordshire, Derbyshire, Warwickshire and Leicestershire come together. Some pubs get their names by accident. An amusing example of this can be seen in the former **Royal Oak** at Westbury-on-Trym, near

Unusual Signs

Bristol. Several years ago the sign was removed and the villagers hung a mouse in its place. The house became known unofficially as the **Mouse** and eventually the owners were obliged to change the name officially.

Young's, the London brewers once named a pub after one of their employees. On the ancient highway, Watling Street, at Rainham Mark, Kent, stands the **Belisha Beacon Inn**, honouring a former Secretary of State and ardent road safety supporter, Leslie Hore-Belisha. When opened in 1938 the inn was the first of its kind to be named in honour of a living notability.

The former **Red Lion** near Iver, Bucks, was renamed the **Gurkha** as a tribute to the soldiers who have maintained a close link with Britain for over 170 years.

The uncoveted honour of unfriendliest pub must go to a pub in Glencoe, Scotland which exhibited a sign for a number of years – **No Campbells.**

Bibliography

There are a number of excellent reference books providing further information on the subject of pubs and pub signs. They include:

Trade Signs and their Origins. C. A. Meadows. Routledge & Kegan Paul. 1957.

Inns, Ales & Drinking Customs of Olde England. F. W. Hackwood. T. Fisher Unwin. 1909.

Elizabethan Life in Town & Country. M. St. Clare Byrne. Methuen. 1925.

Chaucer and his England. G. G. Coulton. Methuen. 1908.

English Social History. Trevelyan. Longman. 1958.

Travel in the 17th Century. J. Parkes. Oxford University Press. 1933.

History of English Ale and Beer. C. A. Monckton. Longman. 1966.

Johnson's England. Vols. 1 & 2. Edited by A. S. Turberville. Clarendon Press. 1933.

Shakespeare's England. Vols. 1 & 2. Clarendon Press. 1916.

The English Inn. D. Batchelor. Batsford. 1963.

Old Inns of England. W. Gaunt. Batsford. 1958.

Egon Ronay's Pub Guide. The Gas Council/Hutchinson. 1969.

Inn Signs: Their History and Meaning. The Brewers' Society. 1969.

Discovering Inn Signs. Cadbury Lamb and Gordon Wright. Shire Publications. 1968.

Pub Index